I0518538

ESSENTIAL WORKERS

Poems by

MICHAEL POAGE

Spartan
Press

Spartan Press
Kansas City, Missouri
spartanpresskc.com

Spartan
Press

Copyright © Michael Poage, 2025

First Edition: 1 3 5 7 9 10 8 6 4 2

ISBN: 979-8-89975-006-9

LCCN: 2025938374

Author photo: Michael Poage

All rights reserved. No part of this publication may be
reproduced or transmitted in any form or by any means,
electronic or mechanical, including photocopying,
recording or by info retrieval system, without prior
written permission from the author.

Acknowedgements:

Special thanks to the editors of these publications where
some of these poems originally appeared:

Gasconade Review: i was the kid, Discretization techniques,
OLD TOWN, L.A., BE THE TROUBLES.
Midwest: AN OLDER MAN, BREATHING LESSONS.

Table of Contents

If you met them early,
you would recognize them by an absence
of shadow.

-R. S. Thomas, OUT THERE

Again, to the disappeared.

ESSENTIAL WORKERS

ESSENTIAL WORKERS

No one wants to be around anymore.
I just don't have any vivid memories
Recognizing a halt or a sublime
Performance…some idea like the
Invasion of the beauty spring in the languaging
Of the mouth and the languishing
When we can. Circe may be around
The corner, around the bed. She might want
To be with you with her own visiting
Memories. Welcome traveler. My promise
If you sleep with me, is clean soft sheets and sublimity.

RED WHEAT

These are some of those things:
Gradually, the system begins
To break down with ransom,
And capture. Soon the snow, as we
Will see, never measures up to
Expectations. Here in south central,
The meadowlark sits on the remaining
Stone foundation bringing her particular
Ballad to Vermont Street. And the wheat
Being in the ground, red winter
Can begin. It took four days after removing
Life support. Red winter has begun.

LIGHTHOUSE

Ludwig Wittgenstein: *(Philosophical Investigations ix)*
"I should not like my writing to spare other people
the trouble of thinking."

I am not the subject or the
Adjectival reminiscence you may
Be considering in what you say.

My world is a separate one,
Far away from the love of meter
But much closer to loss and the cheater.

Sparse and in between, always in the middle,
Yet another distant twist of sight.
This island, as I am, stands drunk with light.

MY SURROUNDINGS #2

The coffee cup from the underground pottery.
Business in Gaza from 2012. Grounds from today.
My cell phone. Several flash drives,
A small box with business cards, my
Harmonica, a copy of YOU MUST HAVE YOUR
       FAMINE
Leaning against the desk lamp with shade. Several
Pens from plumbing businesses to one I found on the
       sidewalk
In Mostar. I remember trying to give it
To the person who dropped it but I frightened her
With my shouting in English. A Palestinian 2024
Calendar on my closet door as the Israeli massacre is in
Its eighth month. Four manuscripts, my hope for the
       future,
Stacked up on my desk. They are mine waiting in line to
       be sent
Out to a pleasant publisher. Around me photos of my
       children
And grandchildren, a framed painting of a Panda done
       by Cora
In 1985. She was still 3 years old then (5-23-85). Books
Stacked on the floor crawling toward me sideways like
       crabs.
I just learned recently that crabs don't have eyes. Is that
       right?
My books have eyes, they protect my peace. Usually. Along
With some of the books is material I used to officiate at
       the funeral
Of a longtime good friend, a week ago. Like Rev. Thomas,
I write questionable poems about my world and beyond.

TATTOO FROM JERICHO

Subordinate clause upon
subordinate clause. What happened
to the verbs buried
under the tattoos in the soul,
legacy of the father,
their drifting daughters
being obstacles to the joy
bouncing around one or another toy.

Daytona condensed converted into energy
as the fulfillment of walking up
from Jericho to our vocabulary
far from that of John Knox, the danger
of that couple embracing in plain sight
and the laughter allowed only at night.

IN THE SILENCE

In the silence of the moment
After the last breath
The old man holds her hand,
Strokes her face. In the silence
After a long while her skin
Begins to cool, a temperature
Not even their favorite old blanket
Can warm back to normal. The old man
Feels like a prisoner chained to the wrong side
In the silence of the moment after. It's a
Decadent world making her skin forever cold,
Stealing her from him, closing the door forever cold.
The old man rolls over in the bed and faces the wall.

THE ROOD

my copper bracelet shades the skin green
as the krakening sky boasts death to the wanderers
and we all claim to be the most sick
as in no one has more serious symptoms
than any of you I can always top you
with my pain my tumors my skin rashes
pain in my head that is I am sure trigeminal
neuralgia the suicide disease which is why
the rood is over my door no one else deserves it

EXCAVATION

"The first major excavations in decades shed light on how ordinary citizens shopped and snacked—and where slaves slept." --- Rebecca Mead

Pompeii still holds buried secrets
Like you and me, our neighbors,
The dead from the Balkan wars and
Our parents, also buried or
Scattered. Every loss, soft and alive,
Reveals more loss, reveals nuclear-
Laced shrapnel that surfaces as winter's
Rain opens bereavement. It's smooth
And slippery this consistency of life.

i was the kid

who hid
in the arts
and crafts closet
in eighth grade

it was dance time
in physical education
which terrified me
dancing
and being educated
physically

HEAT

In this heat
the cats are drinking
more water from
the birdbaths
than the birds.

And they are not
your cats. But then,
they are not
your birds
either.

Discretization techniques

i thought it was
a typo at first
a word I had
never seen but
sounds like the focal
name for some
inquisitional torture
turns out it is
a part of the
vocabulary of mathematics
not sure what it
means never knew
anything about
mathematics next
day no reason just
a quiet drain of
water or the blood
of your people
mixed with the ashes
of your village wherever
the location of such
techniques it will
always be discretization

OLD TOWN, L.A.

Yes, I know that, she said
While staring off into some
Scream coming from the planet
Called Venus. She felt compelled
To get there and find out why
The disturbance. She walked
Into Union Station here in L.A.'s
Old Town. I stood outside in
The fool's gold light of this
August near Chavez. I got
Worried having let her out of
My sight. In her manic
Mood she will spread her
Wings and dance with anyone
And her advantage would be gone.
So, find her I said, I know that, she said.

GROUND TRUTH

If the system breaks down
think of it as an optical
illusion or a lie. Then you
throw out all the items
with the "use before" outdated
by over five years. International
law prevails here as much as at
The Hague. Love struggles
by the handbook but still
was overcome by the will
to be the bad-ass and ignore
the "forever" on the stamp.

Maybe it was distrust
or fear or forgotten taste
that provoked "use before"
or "forever," surrender
to the ground truth, the
illusion, that ONE lie.

LAST SUPPER IN RAFAH

For Rachel Corrie

You hear the Holy Qur'an
like Lorca heard the sky
or the shaking ground. Please bless
this step, and the next one. From your window
anything Holy is everything unless it is disrupted
by what we call a mistake, or intentional
crushing death by something yellow from
America. You hear the Holy Qur'an and
the Advent stories of the birth this season in the gospel
    myth
of September 15, the truth like an avalanche everyone
    can see
exploding in front of them. But soon your entire village
    is overwhelmed
by the King's men slaughtering all the children under two
years. How does knowledge start with a question and
    come back to
another one? Szymborska proclaims the sky
and the trembling ground, you hear the words that
    embrace your village
before the last nightly reading of the Holy Qur'an
like Lorca heard the sky, like you heard the village mothers
scream in lament.

READ THE ROOM

In your eloquence
you capture the attention
then the devotion
of the state of Louisiana.

You speak of the sky
and water, breathing
and waiting. Names
of prior devotees of the state
are etched into the wall
you gaze toward and dream
of the horizon of the Gulf
and breaking out of this room,
since childhood, with hot sauce
tending the kitchen table.

We could go laugh at the poets
near the park, sing the harp
till the adults sleep, read
the room without the nurturing
scream of obscene miscalculation,
but for now, I feel like a passenger
in my own body.

NOW EYES CLOSED

The tool of moaning for the man.
                    Entanglements,
now smiling,
                now eyes closed.
A photograph is always
a glance at the real, the moan,
                the sterile.
Pleasant
            magnum of abundance as we promised,
A silence like brothers,
Committing to each other,
                With the sad love of blood.

THE SWEET GUM TREE

The challenge is to walk
barefoot on the grass after the seed pods
have fallen to the ground. The naked feet
are in the wrong war. Or perhaps
it's a kind of intimate ritual
to touch pain, the familiar,
the comfort place with spots
of blood on the sidewalk
sweet as sweet could be.

WALL CLOUD WRITING

Explain your gladness,
the ancient dark
desperate grasses of

the high plains,
sweetgrass to Canada.

And her celebrity with
books and brains
speaking all those
black volumes on
the shelf.

Bly could work up
a
dance with drums,
anxious and

               cold
as the winter

wall cloud, holding her pen
like the Chilean poet

along the front range
as long as the continents

embrace her with love
and her wall cloud writing.

the cross

1.

Do your winter
in the next room
or on the balcony.
Those pills are meant
to reduce depression
which is why
the "anti" is on
the label. Why do
you name your dogs
after ex-boyfriends?
Max, Bob, Luis....

2.

One of my daughters
had a nightmare
when she was younger:
she saw me
crucified on a cross.
She just recently told me.

3.

Nothing to do with boyfriends
or ex-dogs.

BIRTH CANAL

This is the natural
aggression of things,
going from one life
to another, left
to become her secret
near the garden –
of ask, old trees
behind the steel
factory to become
his secret and together
they plan this natural
aggression of things
falling from limb to limb
born out of drunkenness.

MONOGRAPH

She and sadness have been
on my mind. It is now
published as a monograph
like an invisible storm
studied all her life. It can
be both terrifying and strange
depending on how you read
the original or the translation,
the tongue or the mind. Sweet
skin of the page, a number
to go by, beautiful plots
under a tree, as the anxious
widow-to-be explains to us
the best way for him to go, asleep
like an obscure monograph.

THE FASCIST ENTERTAINER

Christmas, 2016

The cheese and crackers are ornamental only.
The very unique and delicious-looking chips
are forbidden. We are in dangerous
culinary-political territory. She
means the delightful words
she doesn't say and her actions, flanking
maneuvers, will lead us as unwitting
combatants, to a mouth-watering ambush,
we'll lose half our company to the holiday ice,
the unplowed roads, fresh New England snow.
I have not had time to study the enemy and don't
remember her at the beautiful wedding although
I am told I spoke to her – she is that good. I am
afraid of stepping on the landmines so
temptingly arranged, delicately placed, almost
hidden, sliced, magazine-style, take-a-photo
Chelsea before the Stutka's find us out in
the open and we have another Leningrad.
My naiveté about family sneak attacks
and double and triple betrayals in a few short
years ends suddenly with the still controversial
use of a weapon introduced to humanity
vaporizing all especially the innocent.

Driving between things to do

You spit the words out
thinking it will make
me pay more attention.
But I only turn away at

the display of anger and
you drive on, with the grind
of suffering, the tension at the neck,
all that is lost between things to do.

VETERAN

mid-spine

shattered

hollow point
made jello

of bone

my bone

my innocent, not so, bone

was 6 feet 2 inches
now,
in this chair,

3 feet 10 inches

waiting for white
chickens on red
wheelbarrow

to look up at me in my window
tell me what to do next

and how.

FATHERHOOD

From the foreclosed
Dairy farm in eastern
Colorado my father
Emerged at fourteen
Into a bowl of dust working
To get to Kansas City
And drifting back west
To Almena for high school,
Football and a sweetheart.
How could he know
The next decades of war and
Whiskey? Working for the funeral
Home, school classes and called to
Accident sites to retrieve
Body parts. There's no way
He could have known
Or changed much as
His family split up into many
Directions disappearing through
The clouds covering the storms
In the Rockies. The farm
With only grass growing
Taller than even the corn
And the south wind
Scraping chips of lead paint
Off the house now leaning
Toward the dark ground.
Sleeping at the funeral home
How could he know
Who would climb
And who would fall?

CHRISTMAS, PHILADELPHIA:
SUBURBAN STATION

I walked past some famous downtown park on my way to
Suburban Station. 30th Street Station wasn't too far but
    the
opening scene to the movie, Witness, was filmed in one
    of
the men's rooms there. I saw it – or maybe it was the one.

So I stayed away, maybe superstitious, or just fuckin
    scared,
especially having just visited Christmas and in-laws, we
    were
now headed for the airport with ice storms and blizzards
    laying
down their wonderland in the Midwest as our destination

froze. We had all our stuff, my duffle bag, my wife had
    her
roller bag as she walked about a block ahead of me. My
    left
damn knee was screaming so I could not walk as fast.
    What
the hell? As usual I am following, down the escalator to
    the

train level. With my duffle bag strapped over my shoulder
I held the door open for people slower even than me.
    Got
directions to the waiting area for the airport train and sat
    down
on the cold, iron bench. I stretched my legs out and put
my

feet on top of the bag for security and comfort, crossed my arms over my favorite red sweater and pulled my cap down. The train instantly arrived but all I saw was a large, black man standing in front of me with a sign that told me where I could

get a warm meal. "Homeless, too" was at the top of the sign. I knew my wife was calling me to come to the train but all I heard was this bear of a man agreeing with me about how hard it was bein' homeless. Brother, he said, nice sweater, keeps you warm

for a while. I was being visited by Christmas, told where I could get a hot meal, made sure I knew the location, just around the corner. Then he put out his Ali fist, and we connected with a
    bump.
I watched him go over to someone curled up on the cold, hard

concrete a few feet away. He must have read the words on the baseball cap my son had given to me from his work on a movie crew in Austin. He must have read the words and knew my hunger: "The Long Road Home." And he heard my silence.

BREATHING LESSONS

You could start by
    listening
           to
    Coltrane's
"Living Space"
             taking a deep breath

before swallowing
blood

my heart is considering the sea,
contain your crazy loss. One student
        named Rose
        who is Muslim spoke

with a gentle voice, breath by breath
        then we turned to
                Coltrane
and asked for "Living Space."

BETTER REFRAIN FROM CAUSING A STINK

There are the smug who live through
their attitude and the egotistical
who offend with cowardly ranting.

I have spoken at forums on creativity
and officiated at funerals for
teenagers shot dead by gang rules.

I drove my great uncle's 1915
Pierce Arrow to his grave at Mt. Hope
Cemetery, then auctioned it the next day.

I refereed a junior high basketball game
in a community gym in Ovando, Montana's
winter, twenty below, the crowd on the edge

of life with Peppermint Schnapps being passed
around better than the basketball. The parents
and drunk ranch hands didn't like some of

my calls, yelled at me and threw
the ball at my head when it bounced into
the bleachers. The players were getting

frustrated with so many adults screaming
so, I stopped the game cold and told the crowd
to leave the gym, only players, coaches and

officials could stay. They all obeyed, cleared
the gym swearing and grumbling. I resumed the game,
wondered about my after-game life in overtime.

AN OLDER MAN

Fifty years later, following some death,
I arranged for the fate
of my next five. I consciously opened
my soul's cousin
and was told I could now only sing solo.

BE THE TROUBLES

What does a soul smell like?
There have been relatively few
academic papers or international
conferences in Ljubljana or
elsewhere on this subject. Be the troubles
imagined with the swill of research
into heaven and hell just seeking evidence.

BARELY DIVINE

You have helped so many
Cross the bridge
As every moment is filled with days
Worth of blame
And Baroque or Romantic.
Remember that the English
Grammar School does not mean
English Grammar but "Latin" School
For the sake of advancing. You schooled yourself
And it wasn't in Latin or the fine details
Of any grammar. You have been working on your first
    symphony
Without a morning meal so the notes are music
Filled with hunger and nostalgia for travel
And begged food. You are into your manic
Phase, throw off your clothes, and feel barely divine.

BEDTIME STORY

The lips of love and blood
born into the straw
floor while you imagine
a life of full memory
--- again, threadbare ---
unlike the plastic
inserted into the lifeline
pounding, a drum, a war
completes this bedtime story.

VIGIL/VIGILANT/VIGILANTE

Caught in the current of Furnace Creek
you soon know your breathing is clumsy
and you are out of strength to maintain
a specific course on the water. Side to side,
rock against rock all the finer points of life
are passing you by. It becomes a Polanski
film of one French survivor as the title of
this poem shows: Vigil/Vigilant/Vigilante/
pushes you to make decisions about meaning and
surviving the vertigo moment to moment in the
wake of some lubricious ex-girlfriend of someone
you know or want to be. How is your voice at this
point in the journey? Are you keeping an eye out
for the confluence of Prison Creek you noticed
on the map ages ago? Your body is sacred and any
forgiveness must be accepted by him. The ache
in your stomach is the stress of controlling the title
of this poem: Vigil/Vigilant/Vigilante. Your body
should be worshipped instead of being ignored by
a draining embrace and fear, that's it, fear
of being called addict, lost, spider. You ask
yourself, 'Why didn't I hire that guide who knows
these creeks like his scarred face?' but it is
too late to be safe. Love's mystery leads you
through this long-distance flight in the waters so
you set to work on another climax hoping to be
rescued by the pleasure and the ambition of your
caress but it all devolves into the disappeared
of South American countries, Mexico for instance. O
taste and be bought by someone for five loaded rifles
and the title of this poem: Vigil/Vigilant/Vigilante.

TEXAS SONNET

When I started school
there was no gun
class, though I've heard
of them. This was Miami,
Texas, the Panhandle,
and there was one cop
for the whole county,
Roberts, population 1001.

My dad discovered several men
just refused to own a gun,
WWII had left an impression.
They'd had enough of killing.
And that cop. He was legally
blind. His wife drove him on patrol.

GOODBYE

Your voice is less
and less heard. Why
do you become more
quiet each day? You say
it is me. Rather you
whisper, move your lips
with barely any expulsion
of air. Like a pers
on, held
in my arms, dying. It is
no secret that the pressure
on your heart has been
like this for years and you
have tried so many ways
to live right. I'll stroke your
hair, thinned by age, I'll
stroke your hair, whisper in
your ear, we will all be fine.

THE CHANT

No one knows the meaning
of the words. Just
listen. Swallow
the sound. Do not
pray, it brings too
much intention
into the beauty. Make
a small cry for
your mother or father
or no one.

PARTNER FOR LIFE

Death is a strange partner
to have and hold. Commitment
is clear from the beginning
as is the breakup.

Whether a civil union, partner
until the end or marriage,
death holds your hand
even if you try to

let go. The more you
argue, the more you lose
ground, so to speak.
Why didn't we divorce years ago?

RADIOLOGY

In the backyard a squirrel
among the academics with books
and chemicals. In the morning
the grass is still wet from my
weekly soaking of the property
but I stop because of the
squirrel and the academics
and because we are in the middle
of a drought so what can
I do. I started work at 2 a.m. to clean
the campus of leaves and MacDonald's cups
and the occasional condom. I am feeling
better even though Mikhail
says, "…poetry is not medicine
--- it's an X ray."

the fall

it's a wary time, a weary time,
but he maintained his resolutions planned
just yesterday but, still planned. he decided
on some specific resolutions that he missed
at the first of the year and now, in
september, has even written some of them
down. however, he has not shown any of them
to me. he is superstitious and believes that
making them public, even to one person, could cause
irreparable damage. And I am good with that. I don't trust
him anyway. he has betrayed me several times
and each time it has cost me my body
and soul, even if it felt good at the time.
it's a wary time, a weary time.

MODULATE

With so many floods
and mudslides

we cannot swallow
anymore. The modulation
of our tongue

is lost in the quiet
of such natural
disasters – regulate

the lips and the teeth,
now adjust

the soft larynx
tissue – lungs fill
full from screaming.

My family
is sweet on small blossoms.

THE CITY OF HEATHROW

On a bus
On the M25 at 6 pm
For Heathrow
Sometimes we move
And sometimes
We move

PYRAMID DOG CREEK

So much sand, so little time. The Pyramid Dog Creek
drags its way across the barrenness toward the River
Nile. It is a bitter journey. No one has actually ever
seen this Creek. In fact, it would be called a Wadi if
anyone spotted it. And the real mystery is the legend
of the Pyramid Dog said to be two millennium in the
making. It is gold. It is silver. It has survived inside
Giza and comes out for food at inconvenient times. It
loves to be caressed. It hates all human contact. The
Creek is usually dry as a Wadi is usually dry, hiding its
water below the grit and sting of the desert. It is true –
everything about the Pyramid Dog.

I don't remember

Is it feed a cold
Starve a fever or
The other way?
It's like snow
In October. I don't
Remember last
October except that
I was in another
Country. That's all.

THE WET MOUNTAINS

And from there we went by horse along the foothills
    keeping an eye out above and below
For friend or not. We still never saw what hit us. Using
    this very plain English I describe
To you the, the power and the only love we ever saw in
    the years we rode from east to
West, north to south. War after war no peace was ever
    like what we experienced through
These mountains, these stars, thousands of stars in a
    night so dark, so cold, from each
Speck of light we all heard the scream breaking the
    night into glass, shattered like water
Slicing us, using our own skin for its scattered, washed
    in the wet blood, demoned passion.

KINLOSS ABBEY

A gloss of black
birds circled the abbey.
A man walked out of
the graveyard
for veterans
of some unstated
conflict. It is the only
part of the abbey
not in ruins. He carried
a camera, said he was
shooting for a possible
Halloween event. The rhythm
of silence welcomes
all to enjoy the sacramental
ghosts, a picnic for public
executions. Even in these ruins
the silent drop of the ax
urges caution, polite
bows to the whispering wind
of Kinloss Abbey, key
in the ignition and a Trappist
departure toward the paved road.

DON'T VARY THE KEY

Have you opened the
door for anyone
today? My grandfather, the
musician and
painter of U.S.
midwestern diners
and movie theatres,
and an alcoholic,
really didn't know
what to expect.
[He also illustrated covers
for Western magazines]
But neither did his only
daughter, home-coming
queen in northwest
Kansas. She was soon
to face a world of war
with me in the mix.
The reviews in the papers
the next day were very
favorable but one critic
wrote about the monotone
and clumsy key changes.
The one rankled remark
sent the family weeping,
drinking, veiled into
the night. Vary the key,
he said, and lock the door
behind you.

I LEAVE PIECES OF MYSELF

I leave pieces of myself
All over the house.
Yesterday I lost my
left thumb for hours
until I found it in the
freezer's ice container
and put it back on my hand
sending a sensual chill
up my arm. Several days
ago the watch I bought
for 25 Bosnian Marks
disappeared from my
wrist. I walked around
timeless in a fog much
different that the usual
brain fog containing a sweet
acquaintance with time but
soon the watch was found
behind the faucet on the bathroom
sink, the scuffed shine of the watchband
chameleoned by the dull silver
of the time-sad faucet. Maybe I
am not seeing things as I
used to, can't hold myself
together, or the world, on the
precipice of disaster. I knew
Afghanistan was a mistake, Iraq,
Vietnam, all failures except for the
corrupt corporations and politicians

whose stock, one way or another,
I own and whose dessert I enjoy
on the edge of the desert
next to be damned.

DONATIONS

Here in Carmel finally
The sun.
There have been days
Of fog
From the sea

Shedding a gray light
Across the
Most colorful flowers
In the garden
That doesn't exist

Yet because of my own
Yemeni obsession
With water
Bottles of plastic and empty
Thoughts of feeding

The baby
My own slight flow of urine
As she cries night
After night for a glimpse
Of the plashing peace.

ANOTHER SIEGE

-Mostar 1993-4

That incident
The closing of the door
The ascension of the sniper

( )

Slipping out of something comfortable
Spilling the good Scotch

( )

There are answers, no, not really
But the questions signal

( )

The Goliath of bombed
Schools to come out into
View in the valley of Ilah
One stone

( )

With one stone he falls
As if he was someone great,
Well-known

( )

O, the stone, the artillery
That sends us on the prowl
A search for the potential
Translation from *petros*
To tongue. Why all these questions?
All for the sake of naked truth
Slipped out of something comfortable?
Yes, until nothing else moves.

THE HILL OF MAUD THE SAINT

Threadbare
Around the turn of the year
From the top of the hill
Of St. Maud nothing
Looks familiar
Or close, everything lonely
To the reality of connection.

For Maud, the servant
Of God, the military-industrial
Complex is a severe wound,

You approach the hill
With ice in your legs,
Sainthood as rags
A shaking of the ground
That keeps drawing
And quartering her
Already dead-to-the-wall patients.

Wrapped around your feet.
In fairness and a bleak
Promise in the Scottish bog future
Pray to Saint Maud in your love-less isolation.

SPAM:18834219982

I am reading a Hershfield poem
published in Poetry London
in the quiet of morning:
"Body, mind of the ransacked...."

Then SPAM rings. I rush to the phone
to avoid waking my wife. I pick up the handset,
push TALK, then OFF in quick succession

and it rings again. I push TALK and OFF
to choke the noise out of SPAM.

It is not a ring, more like a machete stabbing through
    the air,
a power drill making a loud hole in the bone of the day.

THE MUSEUM

The first to go is the smile.
Then comes a justification for being late.
Trust erodes with an obvious averting of the eyes.
Real affection then transforms into hugging a sibling.
Finally, recrimination or blame slams the door shut
   behind you.

A WORD HERE

Let's do this small
lyric together. You
think of one word:
_____. Good,
Now I will add,
"throat." Your next
word is: _____.
So I will add, "tree."
And we will go back
and forth like that until
we make a new thing,
and we will have a gift
for each other, we will
stop fighting, everyone
will stop yelling and
shooting and dropping
cluster bombs and using
chemical weapons. We
will share this gift of
gentle words, of poetry
and peace with each
of you gathered around
the world, even just one,
especially even just one.

JACOB BLAKE

Kenosha, 2020

It's a way to bring
us together. The windows
were forever closed but recently
you discovered they would open,
but then…crushing news. The storm
windows are permanent, all of them
across the front of the house. As we
continue living so close and growing
away, we cannot stand the
rambling in Russian as he claimed,
as he claimed to make it a joke. It really
means, as we look around, that many
of our friends, even us, are facing ---
as Blake said, just like THAT, snapping his
fingers --- disability, loss of legs or speech
or "I don't know who you are," by bullet
or brain. Then, a lifetime of wandering begins again.

PLAGARISM

As I mentioned, the pain
hasn't stopped me. I
even read your letter,
so good to see your hand-
writing. I remember the day
I gave you that Kunitz
book. The cover had a life
size hand silhouette. You
put your hand on the
book. I put my hand on
yours. It was a hard cover
first edition, a perfect and solid
landing place for our life to
be strong and safe, a foundation
for a new world of imitation.

SQISHY POSTPARTEUM
STOMACH

I can't help it!
The flesh will be
The flesh. My three
Year old son likes
To knead it – bread
For the wilderness.
Or a way for him
To claim part of me
For himself since
The breasts now feed
His fifteen month old
Sister. Really, he is not
Jealous, maybe curious
Like my husband
About what comes next.

WHENEVER I STEP

Whenever I step out of my front door
the dog across the street, behind
a gate, barks and barks as if
I am challenging its life on this
earth. Just vicious attempts
to do the most to hold on to minority
power, just old-fashioned evil.

Then you tell me about the world's
first space hotel, ready for occupancy
in 2027. I respond with, "Ok, but
how will the hot tub work?" In the
grey dusk of a coming storm – my
real question – as the horizon begins
to disappear, is just that. In six
years, will that horizon have already
taken me in, introduced me around?

ROCKS

I went for a walk with my mom.
We went into the wilderness.
There was a river, rocks to throw
And rocks too heavy to lift.
I like home with my mom.
I am young but I know enough.

MAWKISH

What is the difference
between forever and
eternity? A long amount
of time, or no time, fighting
island to island, so it is.

War is present tense, not passive,
to you. No "remember when"
while drinking with buddies
at the officer's club, so it is,
fighting island to island.

Remember, you will be
in very limited fashion
at the end
of the day. At the end of the year.
At the end. So it is.

CUPIDITY

Go into the thin blue air
with all your years
and wings unknown
to those below. Be the acrobat

that moves in oblique
circles and surrounds the clouds
with crystals of yourself
bonding together

making you be the someone
who would like to do this
with him, into the thin blue air
you acrobat your heart's message.

BREATH AND PARTICLES

She allowed herself
one breath
having been told
the particles were not
interested in mothers.
She blushed. She remembered

leaving him to elude
honesty, maybe: 'I have no idea'
was her first statement
when he asked: 'Of all people,'
he said in return: 'Well,'

she replied, 'I have a slight
idea. Yes, like breath
and particles,
a slight idea.'

BIRDS AND WALES

Through the window
I watch sea birds fly over
the roof tops. I am living
in a 17th century fishing village
on the north coast of Scotland.

It is mid-September
and the sea is contemplating
its next move. Then a friend
whom I had never met
took the train from Wales

arriving on my doorstep
just in time.

Michael Poage was born in Virginia. He has published fifteen books of poetry, most recently, *HEART: COLLECTED POEMS* 1975-2024, Spartan Press, 2024. He served as the Poet-in-Residence at Dzemal Bijedic University in Mostar, Bosnia & Herzegovina, 2018, and has taught English literature and ESL courses in Bosnia and Herzegovina, the U.S., Latvia and, virtually, in Thailand. He lives in Wichita, Kansas with his wife, the historian, teacher, activist, and writer Dr. Gretchen Eick.

This project was made possible, in part, by generous support from the Osage Arts Community.

Osage Arts Community provides temporary time, space and support for the creation of new artistic works in a retreat format, serving creative people of all kinds — visual artists, composers, poets, fiction and nonfiction writers. Located on a 152-acre farm in an isolated rural mountainside setting in Central Missouri and bordered by ¾ of a mile of the Gasconade River, OAC provides residencies to those working alone, as well as welcoming collaborative teams, offering living space and workspace in a country environment to emerging and mid-career artists. For more information, visit us at www.osageac.org

Osage Arts Community

www.ingramcontent.com/pod-product-compliance
Lightning Source LLC
Chambersburg PA
CBHW031248120626
46545CB00007B/2702